MISS MOORE
THOUGHT OTHERWISE

How Anne Carroll Moore Created Libraries for Children

Written by JAN PINBOROUGH

Illustrated by DEBBY ATWELL

Houghton Mifflin Books for Children
HOUGHTON MIFFLIN HARCOURT
Boston New York 2013

Once in a big house in Limerick, Maine, there lived a little girl named Annie Carroll Moore. She had large gray eyes, seven older brothers, and ideas of her own.

In the 1870s many people thought a girl should stay inside and do quiet things such as sewing and embroidery.

But Annie thought otherwise. She preferred taking wild toboggan rides from the cemetery all the way down past Main Street, or bouncing along in Father's buggy to the sound of Pocahontas's clip-clopping hooves.

Through the trees Annie could glimpse the White Mountains, far away in the distance. She dreamed about the world that lay beyond—and about what she would do someday.

Annie loved the stories and poems Father read aloud
to her after dinner. On rainy afternoons, she would
climb up to the attic to look at a children's magazine
called *St. Nicholas*.

In those days, children weren't allowed to go inside
libraries. People didn't think reading was very important
for children—especially not for girls.

When Annie turned nineteen, many girls her age were already married.

Back then, an unmarried girl like Annie might keep house for her parents, or perhaps become a teacher or a missionary.

But Annie thought otherwise. She decided to become a lawyer like her father, and day after day she went to his law office to learn how.

Then in one terrible week, Annie's parents both died from the flu. When her brother's wife died too, Annie stayed home to take care of her two little nieces. Venturing beyond the White Mountains would have to wait.

After several years, her brother married again, and Annie heard exciting news. Libraries were hiring women as *librarians!* Annie packed her bags and traveled to Brooklyn, New York, to enroll in the Pratt Institute library school.

New York was a big city. Some people thought it was a dangerous place for a young woman to live on her own.

But Annie thought otherwise. She loved walking along its busy cobblestone streets, going to the circus and the opera, and riding in a horse-drawn car across the great Brooklyn Bridge.

Annie studied hard. She graduated from library school and got her first job as a librarian at the Pratt Free Library. Some libraries were beginning to let children come inside, but Annie's library had something brand new—a library room planned just for children. Children could come in and take books off the shelves. And in the evenings Annie read aloud to them—just as her father had read to her.

Word spread about Annie's library until one day a man named Dr. Bostwick asked her to be in charge of *all* the children's sections in the thirty-six branches of the New York Public Library.

Miss Moore dressed in her finest hat and suit and visited each library, from Harlem to Chatham Square.

She saw that many librarians did not let children touch the books, for fear that they would smudge their pages or break their spines. They thought if children were allowed to take books home, they would surely forget to bring them back.

But Miss Moore thought otherwise. She trusted children, so she created a big black book with this pledge inside:

When I write my name in this book
I promise to take good care of the book I use
at home and in the library,
and to obey the rules of the library.

Miss Moore persuaded the librarians to use this pledge so *all* the children of New York could check out books and take them home.

Miss Moore pushed for other changes, too. She urged the librarians to take down the SILENCE signs and spend time talking with children and telling them stories.

She pulled dull books off the shelves and replaced them with exciting ones such as *The Adventures of Tom Sawyer* and *The Swiss Family Robinson*.

She wrote book reviews and made book lists to help parents, librarians, and teachers find good books for children—and to encourage book publishers to publish better children's books.

But many libraries still kept children's books locked in cabinets or tucked away in corners. They did not have enough books for children or enough shelves to put them on.

So when it was announced that a grand new library would be built on Fifth Avenue and Forty-Second Street, Miss Moore was determined to make its new Central Children's Room the best it could be for all the children of New York.

Miss Moore had child-size tables and chairs specially made. She chose beautiful pictures by N. C. Wyeth and other artists to hang on the walls.

For the floors, she found rosy pink tiles
from Wales.

She gathered collections of shells and butterflies
to display. Then she filled the shelves with the very
best children's books she could find.

Finally, one warm spring day in 1911, the huge bronze
doors of the New York Public Library swung open for the
first time.

Crowds lined the streets as a police escort brought
the president of the United States, William Howard Taft,
to dedicate the magnificent new library.

When the library opened to the public the next day, the children of New York City walked through their own special entrance into the new Children's Room. Hundreds of new children's books in many languages waited within reach. And beneath every window, a cozy window seat waited for children to curl up in it.

From then on, every day seemed to hold a new surprise in the Children's Room. Miss Moore organized reading clubs and invited musicians, storytellers, and famous authors like Dr. Seuss to entertain the children.

Often, Miss Moore would reach into her handbag and pull out a wooden doll named Nicholas Knickerbocker. Children who were just learning English felt less shy about talking when Nicholas was around.

One day the king and queen of Belgium visited the New York Public Library. "You *must* come see the Children's Room," Miss Moore told the queen. That day all the children in the library—from the richest to the poorest—shook hands with a king and queen.

Outside the library walls, two world wars, epidemics, and the Great Depression came and went. But inside, the Children's Room was always warm and bright—a place where children could meet other children and learn interesting things.

In big cities and small towns across America, more and more libraries began to copy Miss Moore's Central Children's Room. So did libraries in England, France, Belgium, Sweden, Russia, India, and Japan.

When Miss Moore turned
seventy years old, it was time for
her to retire.
Some people thought she
should sit quietly at home.
But Miss Moore
thought otherwise.
Her friends at the
library gave her a set
of luggage—with a
small green suitcase
for Nicholas—and
she traveled across
the country,
teaching more
people how to
make good
libraries for
children.

Today libraries across America have thousands of books for children. And thanks to the help of a little girl from Limerick, Maine, who had ideas of her own, any child can choose a book from a library shelf, curl up in a comfortable seat to look through it— and then take it home to read.

The children of this world will never be able to repay the debt they owe [Anne Carroll Moore].

—WALTER DE LA MARE

MORE ABOUT MISS MOORE

TRAILBLAZING LIBRARIANS

ANNE CARROLL MOORE DID NOT singlehandedly create the children's library. A group of strong pioneering women librarians around the country also helped blaze the trail.

* In 1887, Minerva Sanders created a children's area in a public library in Pawtucket, Rhode Island.

* In 1894, the Milwaukee librarian Lutie Stearns gave a speech calling for children of all ages to be allowed in libraries.

* In 1896, at the Pratt Institute, Mary Wright Plummer opened the first library room designed specifically for children and gave Miss Moore free rein to implement her ideas, including the first version of the famous library pledge.

* In 1904, Caroline M. Hewins, who had campaigned for free libraries, opened a children's library room in Hartford, Connecticut.

* In 1914, the Brooklyn librarian Clara Hunt designed a branch library just for children.

Early children's library rooms were sprinkled around the country in Brookline, Boston, and Cambridge, Massachusetts; Denver; Omaha; Seattle; New Haven; Detroit; and Pittsburgh.

But Miss Moore's unique combination of intelligence, imagination, and ambition—coupled with her connections with authors, illustrators, and publishers and her situation at the iconic New York Public Library—gave her an especially wide-ranging influence in the development of children's library services throughout the country and around the world.

If [the children's] room is now filled with much more sunshine, gaiety, beauty and common sense than ever before it is mainly through the efforts of Annie Carroll Moore who opened wide the windows and said, "A little less stuffiness right here would surely do none of us any harm."

—INSCRIPTION IN *CHRISTMAS CAROLS* BY HENDRIK WILLEM VAN LOON AND GRACE CATAGNETTA

MORE BOOKS, PLEASE!

IN 1880, WHEN ANNE CARROLL MOORE was nine years old, the library in her hometown of Limerick, Maine, was just a rented room in a business building next door to her father's law office. Like many libraries of the time, it had some books for older boys, but not very many for girls or younger children.

Anne at seven.

Many early libraries were not free and open to the public. Sometimes a wealthy person would donate a collection of books and people would pay a membership fee for the privilege of reading them. Often, these collections did not have many books for children.

At a time when few people thought children's books were very important, Miss Moore took them seriously, helping fill library shelves with more and better books for children. In 1904, she prepared a pamphlet called "A List of Books Recommended for a Children's Library." She had strong opinions about books and was never shy about expressing them. Her book reviews appeared in the *Horn Book, Bookman,* and the *New York Herald Tribune.*

Miss Moore befriended and encouraged many important authors and illustrators. Marcia Brown and Eleanor Estes worked in the New York Public Library before they began writing books. Carl Sandburg, Ludwig Bemelmans, and Theodor Geisel paid visits to the library for story times and Children's Book Week. Miss Moore visited Beatrix Potter at Hill Top Farm, and many of Miss Moore's literary friends sent doll-size toys to Nicholas. Pamela Travers gave the Mary Poppins umbrella with its carved parrot head handle to the Central Children's Room, where it was kept on display for many years.

Miss Moore wrote several books herself—two books about Nicholas and a book of essays called *My Roads to Childhood.* Her last published work before her death on January 20, 1961, was an introduction to *The Art of Beatrix Potter.*

In memory of my mother, Shirley Ann Conaway, who took me to the library and taught me to think otherwise.
I would like to acknowledge the generous people who understood why Miss Moore's story needed to be told and
helped me tell it: Shauna Cook Clinger, Mary Casanova, Neil Waldman, Jeanne Lamb, Anne Carroll Peterson
Darger, Marcia Brown, Dr. Christine A. Jenkins, Ann Rider, Debby Atwell, and my family.

— JAN PINBOROUGH

Love you, Lincoln.

—DEBBY ATWELL

SOURCES

Brown, Marcia. Interviews. February 2010.

Brunson, Arrin Newton. "Library Pioneer Honored."
  Salt Lake Tribune, December 29, 2004.

Bugbee, Emma. "Anne Carroll Moore and a Doll
  Draw Children to City Libraries." *New York Herald
  Tribune,* December 30, 1940, p. 18.

Jenkins, Christine A. "Children's Services, Public." In
  Encyclopedia of Library History. New York: Garland
  Publishing, 1994.

Lamb, Jeanne, Coordinator of Youth Collections, New
  York Public Library. Interview. August 22, 2008.

Lepore, Jill. "The Lion and the Mouse." *The New Yorker.*
  July 21, 2008.

Lundin, Anne. *Constructing the Canon of Children's
  Literature.* New York: Routledge, 2004.

Marcus, Leonard S. *Minders of Make-Believe: Idealists,
  Entrepreneurs, and the Shaping of American Children's Literature.*
  Boston: Houghton Mifflin Harcourt, 2008.

Miller, Julie. "Anne Carroll Moore: Our First Supervisor of Work with Children," May 1933; rev.
  by Julia Mucci, May 2004. kids.nypl.org/images/acm_portrait.gif.

Moore, Anne Carroll. *My Roads to Childhood: Views and Reviews of Children's Books.* New York:
  Doubleday, Doran and Company, 1939.

New York Public Library. Anne Carroll Moore Papers.

Sayers, Frances Clarke. *Anne Carroll Moore: A Biography.* New York: Simon & Schuster, 1972.

Portrait of Anne Carroll Moore as a young woman.

Text copyright © 2013 by Jan Pinborough | Illustrations copyright © 2013 by Debby Atwell

Houghton Mifflin Books for Children is an imprint of Houghton Mifflin Harcourt Publishing Company.

www.hmhbooks.com

The text of this book is set in Dante MT.
The illustrations are acrylic on paper.

Library of Congress Cataloging-in-Publication Control Number 2012018092

ISBN 978-0-547-47105-1

Manufactured in China | SCP 10 9 8 7 6 5 4 3 2 1 | 4500386996